D0912898

INSIDE THE NBA

CLEVELAND CAVALIERS

3:31
12

CAVALIERS
23

Sam Moussavi and Samantha Nugent

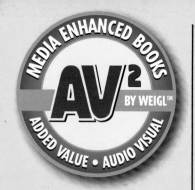

AV² provides enriched content that supplements and complements this book. Weigl's AV² books strive to create inspired learning and engage young minds in a total learning experience.

Your AV² Media Enhanced books come alive with...

Audio
Listen to sections of the book read aloud.

Key Words
Study vocabulary, and complete a matching word activity.

Go to **www.av2books.com**, and enter this book's unique code.

Video
Watch informative video clips.

Quizzes
Test your knowledge.

BOOK CODE

Z 2 6 6 7 6 7

Embedded Weblinks
Gain additional information for research.

Slide Show
View images and captions, and prepare a presentation.

AV² by Weigl brings you media enhanced books that support active learning.

Try This!
Complete activities and hands-on experiments.

... and much, much more!

Published by AV² by Weigl
350 5th Avenue, 59th Floor
New York, NY 10118
Website: www.av2books.com

Library of Congress Control Number: 2016935095

ISBN 978-1-4896-4681-1 (Hardcover)
ISBN 978-1-4896-4682-8 (Multi-user eBook)

Printed in the United States of America in Brainerd, Minnesota
1 2 3 4 5 6 7 8 9 0 20 19 18 17 16

082016
200516

Project Coordinator Heather Kissock
Art Director Terry Paulhus

Photo Credits
Every reasonable effort has been made to trace ownership and to obtain permission to reprint copyright material. The publishers would be pleased to have any errors or omissions brought to their attention so that they may be corrected in subsequent printings.

Weigl acknowledges Newscom, Getty Images, and Alamy as its primary image suppliers for this title.

CLEVELAND CAVALIERS

CONTENTS

Introduction

The Cleveland Cavaliers had been searching for their first National Basketball Association (NBA) Championship win for their entire 46 seasons. The city of Cleveland had not won a major sports championship since 1964. Thanks to Ohio native forward LeBron James, the Cavaliers were able to secure the championship title in 2016, after coming close twice in previous years.

Often scoring more than 20 points per game, power forward and center Kevin Love helped the Cavaliers clinch the number 2 seed in the 2015 NBA Playoffs.

After James left the team in the summer of 2010, the Cavaliers struggled for the next four seasons. The team averaged 24 wins per season and did not qualify for the **playoffs** during that time. The four-year period was the worst in team history. With James' return, the Cavs have proven themselves to be the team to beat in the Eastern **Conference**. Complete with a talented young team, the Cavaliers are working toward achieving another championship in the near future.

CLEVELAND CAVALIERS

Arena Quicken Loans Arena

Division Central Division (Eastern Conference)

Head Coach Tyronn Lue

Location Cleveland, Ohio

NBA Championships 1 (2016)

Nickname(s) Cavs

3 Conference Titles

5 Division Titles

7 Retired Numbers

20 Playoff Appearances

46 NBA Seasons

The Cavaliers acquired Australian-born point guard Kyrie Irving as the first overall draft pick in 2011.

History

The Cavaliers had their highest win percentage of

.805

during the 2008–09 season.

In his career debut for the Cavaliers, Iman Shumpert put up eight points.

The Cleveland Cavaliers joined the NBA as an expansion **franchise** in 1970. The team made its first playoff appearance in 1976 under Coach Bill Fitch. That Cavs squad went to the 1976 Eastern Conference Finals before losing to the Boston Celtics. During the next nine seasons, Cleveland made the playoffs only once. Starting in 1988, Coach Lenny Wilkens led the team to the postseason in four of five seasons, including a conference finals appearance in 1992.

Coach Mike Fratello led the Cavs to the playoffs four times in the mid-1990s, but never past the first round. The franchise struggled until acquiring LeBron James, who had recently graduated from high school, with the first pick in the 2003 NBA Draft. James brought almost instant success to Cleveland, leading the team to its first NBA Finals appearance in 2007. In the summer of 2010, James left Cleveland as a **free agent**.

Before the 2014–15 season, James returned to the Cleveland Cavaliers. The team paired James with young guard Kyrie Irving to give the Cavs two superstar players. That year, the team made it to the NBA Finals for the second time in franchise history.

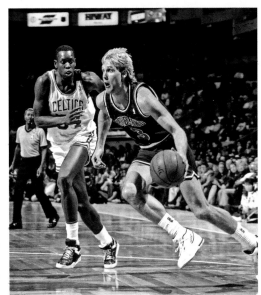

Craig Ehlo played for the Cavaliers from 1986 to 1993. During his 7-season career with the Cavaliers, Ehlo scored 7,492 points.

The Arena

Quicken Loans Arena is the **third-largest** arena in the NBA.

Quicken Loans Arena hosts nearly 2 million guests for more than 200 events each year, including Cavaliers games.

The first home arena in Cleveland Cavaliers history was the Cleveland Arena. The team played there from 1970 to 1974. The Cavaliers did not make the playoffs while playing at the Cleveland Arena. Before the 1974–75 season, Cleveland moved into the Coliseum at Richfield, located in Richfield, Ohio.

Richfield is a suburb of Cleveland, located approximately halfway between Cleveland and Akron. The Cavs played at the Coliseum from 1974 to 1994. The team made its first ever NBA Playoff appearance in 1976 while playing at the Coliseum. In total, Cleveland made 10 playoff appearances, including two Conference Finals, while playing at the Coliseum at Richfield.

Before the 1994–95 season, the Cavaliers moved into the brand new Quicken Loans Arena in downtown Cleveland. The arena was first known as Gund Arena until 2005. Quicken Loans Arena's nickname is "The Q." The team currently plays all of its home games at "The Q." Both NBA Finals appearances took place at the Quicken Loans Arena.

Quicken Loans Arena is home to what is known as the Humungotron, a 5,550-square-foot (1,692-square-meter) LED scoreboard.

Where They Play

British Columbia

Alberta

Ontario

Saskatchewan

Manitoba

CAN

Washington

Montana

North Dakota

Minnesota

7

Wisconsin

25

9

Oregon

Idaho

South Dakota

Iowa

21

Wyoming

Nebraska

Illinois

5

10

UNITED

Nevada

STATES

Utah

Colorado

6

Kansas

Missouri

1

California

2

Arizona

8

Oklahoma

13

Arkansas

3

New Mexico

4

11

Pacific Ocean

MEXICO

Texas

Louisiana

Mis.

15

12

Gulf of Mexico

PACIFIC DIVISION
1. Golden State Warriors
2. Los Angeles Clippers
3. Los Angeles Lakers
4. Phoenix Suns
5. Sacramento Kings

NORTHWEST DIVISION
6. Denver Nuggets
7. Minnesota Timberwolves
8. Oklahoma City Thunder
9. Portland Trail Blazers
10. Utah Jazz

SOUTHWEST DIVISION
11. Dallas Mavericks
12. Houston Rockets
13. Memphis Grizzlies
14. New Orleans Pelicans
15. San Antonio Spurs

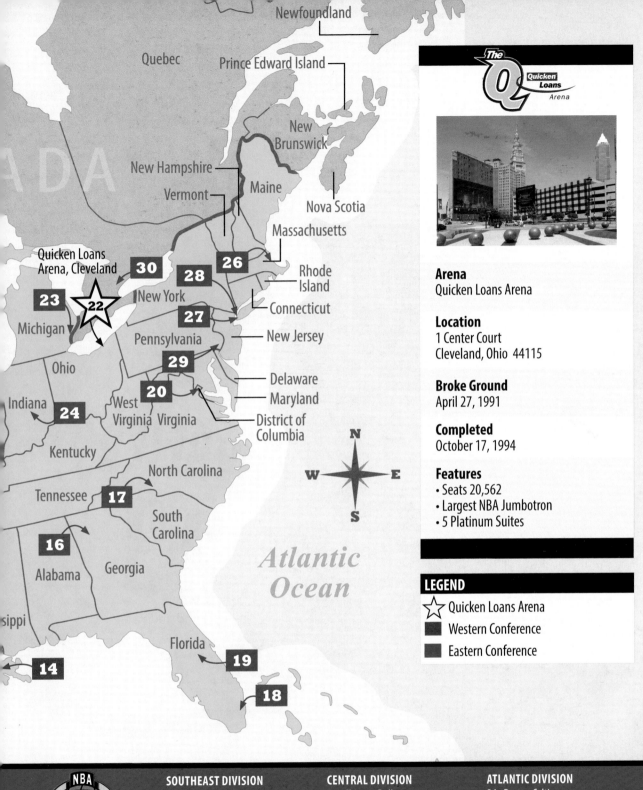

Newfoundland

Quebec

Prince Edward Island

New Brunswick

New Hampshire

Vermont

Maine

Nova Scotia

Massachusetts

Rhode Island

Quicken Loans Arena, Cleveland

30

28

26

23

22

New York

Connecticut

Michigan

27

New Jersey

Ohio

Pennsylvania

29

Delaware

Indiana

24

West Virginia

20

Virginia

Maryland

District of Columbia

Kentucky

North Carolina

Tennessee

17

South Carolina

16

Alabama

Georgia

Atlantic Ocean

N

W   E

S

Florida

19

sippi

14

18

The Q — Quicken Loans Arena

Arena
Quicken Loans Arena

Location
1 Center Court
Cleveland, Ohio 44115

Broke Ground
April 27, 1991

Completed
October 17, 1994

Features
• Seats 20,562
• Largest NBA Jumbotron
• 5 Platinum Suites

LEGEND
☆ Quicken Loans Arena
■ Western Conference
■ Eastern Conference

SOUTHEAST DIVISION
16. Atlanta Hawks
17. Charlotte Hornets
18. Miami Heat
19. Orlando Magic
20. Washington Wizards

CENTRAL DIVISION
21. Chicago Bulls
★ 22. Cleveland Cavaliers
23. Detroit Pistons
24. Indiana Pacers
25. Milwaukee Bucks

ATLANTIC DIVISION
26. Boston Celtics
27. Brooklyn Nets
28. New York Knicks
29. Philadelphia 76ers
30. Toronto Raptors

Cleveland Cavaliers

The Uniforms

6 The Cavaliers played six games in their **"Hardwood Classics"** uniforms in 2015–16.

 The Cavaliers had always used stylized lettering for the "Cavaliers" across the chest. Starting in 2011, they switched to a simpler, block text.

When the Cavaliers franchise joined the NBA, its colors were burgundy and gold. From 1970 to 1981, both the gold home and burgundy away uniforms read "Cavaliers" across the chest. In 1983, the franchise changed its colors to orange, blue, and white. Both the white home and orange away uniforms read "Cavs." From 1987 until 1994, the team's white home uniforms were trimmed in blue, while the blue away uniforms were trimmed in orange.

HOME

AWAY

In 1994, the team's colors were changed to baby blue, orange, and black. Both white home and black away uniforms were trimmed in baby blue. However, in 2003, the team's colors began to shift back to the original color scheme, with burgundy being reintroduced. Since 2010, the colors have been burgundy, navy blue, and gold. The white home uniforms say "Cavaliers" across the chest, and the burgundy away uniforms say "Cleveland".

The Hardwood Classics jersey is a throwback to the jerseys worn by Cavaliers of the 1970s.

The Coaches

The Cavaliers won **66** games during Mike Brown's fourth season as coach in 2008–09.

Cavaliers head coach Tyronn Lue is the youngest active, full-time coach in the NBA.

The Cavaliers franchise has had 20 head coaches in its 46 seasons in the NBA. Seven of those coaches led the team to the NBA Playoffs. Two of those seven, Mike Brown and David Blatt, have led the Cavaliers to the NBA Finals. Former NBA players such as Byron Scott, Keith Smart, and Paul Silas have also coached the team.

BILL FITCH Bill Fitch was the first coach in Cleveland Cavaliers history. Fitch coached the team from 1970 to 1979. He led the franchise to the 1976 Eastern Conference Finals during the Cavs' first postseason appearance. Fitch won 304 regular season games in Cleveland, including 49 in 1975–76, which was a franchise record at the time.

LENNY WILKENS Lenny Wilkens took over as head coach in Cleveland before the 1986–87 season. Wilkens coached the Cavs until 1993, and led the team to five playoff appearances. He is franchise leader in regular season wins, with 316. In 1991–92, Wilkens led Cleveland to 57 wins and the 1992 Eastern Conference Finals.

TYRONN LUE The Cavaliers hired Tyronn Lue as head coach during the 2015–16 season. Lue took over for Coach David Blatt. Before accepting the head coach position with the Cavs, Lue was an assistant coach for the Boston Celtics and Los Angeles Clippers. He played in the NBA for 11 seasons and won two NBA Championships.

The Mascot

Moondog was named after famous Cleveland radio DJ Alan Freed, whose nickname is Moondog.

The Cleveland Cavaliers mascot is named Moondog. Moondog is a large, brown dog that wears a Cavs jersey. He has been the team's official mascot since 2003. Moondog entertains Cavs fans at "The Q" with his acrobatic slam dunks, half-court shots, and pranks on the opposing teams.

Moondog also focuses on his work in the Cleveland community. Each season, he holds the "Moondog 100K Challenge." The program holds a series of walks and runs that Moondog takes part in, along with local students. After each walk or run, he takes time to educate the students about the benefits of keeping active and healthy.

fun facts

#1 Moondog's favorite trick is a behind-the-back half court shot.

#2 In 2003 and in 2004, Moondog was an NBA **All-Star** selection.

Superstars

Many great players have suited up for the Cavaliers. A few of them have become icons of the team and the city it represents.

Larry Nance

Larry Nance was traded to the Cleveland Cavaliers during the 1987–88 season. He played with the Cavs until 1994, when he retired from the NBA. Nance made two NBA All-Star teams and one NBA All-Defensive First Team in Cleveland. He helped the Cavaliers make five playoff appearances, including the 1992 Eastern Conference Finals. Nance held Cavs career averages of 16 points, 8 **rebounds**, and 2 **blocks** per game. His jersey number, 22, was retired by Cleveland on January 30, 1995.

Position: Forward
NBA Seasons: 13 (1981–1994)
Born: February 12, 1959, Anderson, South Carolina, United States

Brad Daugherty

Brad Daugherty attended college at the University of North Carolina at Chapel Hill for four years. Cleveland selected Daugherty with the number one overall pick in the 1986 NBA Draft. He played eight seasons with Cleveland before retiring in 1994 due to back problems. Daugherty was a five-time NBA All-Star and helped the Cavs to five playoff appearances. His final career averages were 19 points, 9 rebounds, and 3 **assists** per game. The Cavaliers retired Daugherty's jersey number, 43, on March 1, 1997.

Position: Center
NBA Seasons: 8 (1986–1994)
Born: October 19, 1965, Black Mountain, North Carolina, United States

Mark Price

Point guard Mark Price was selected in the second round of the 1986 NBA Draft. Price played nine seasons with Cleveland, and made one All-NBA First Team in 1993. He helped the Cavs to seven playoff appearances, including the 1992 Eastern Conference Finals. Price made four All-Star Teams and won two NBA Three Point Shootouts while he was in Cleveland. He finished his Cavaliers career with averages of 16 points and seven assists per game. Price's jersey number, 25, was retired by the Cavs on November 13, 1999.

Position: Point Guard
NBA Seasons: 12 (1986–1998)
Born: February 15, 1964, Bartlesville, Oklahoma, United States

Zydrunas Ilgauskas

Before being drafted by the Cavaliers in 1996, Zydrunas Ilgauskas played professionally in his home country of Lithuania. Ilgauskas joined Cleveland before the 1997–98 season, just one year after he was drafted. He played 12 seasons in Cleveland. Ilgauskas missed the 1999–2000 season due to a severe foot injury. He made six playoff appearances for the Cavs, including the franchise's first NBA Finals in 2007. Ilgauskas held Cavs career averages of 13 points and seven rebounds per game. His jersey number, 11, was retired by Cleveland on March 8, 2014.

Position: Center
NBA Seasons: 13 (1997–1999 and 2000–2011)
Born: June 5, 1975, Kaunas, Lithuanian SSR, Soviet Union

The Greatest of All Time

There are several standout players on the Cavaliers roster who have worked hard to push the team to success. Often, there is one player who has become known as the "Greatest of All Time," or GOAT. This player has gone above and beyond to achieve greatness and to help his team shine.

LeBron James

Position: Small Forward/Power Forward
NBA Seasons: 13 (2003–present)
Born: December 30, 1984, Akron, Ohio, United States

The Cleveland Cavaliers selected LeBron James with the number one pick in the 2003 NBA Draft. James came to the NBA straight out of high school. He was a hometown favorite who had attended St. Vincent–St. Mary High School, in nearby Akron, Ohio. James quickly became a superstar and reversed the fortunes of the Cavs franchise.

From 2005 to 2010, James led Cleveland to five straight playoff appearances, including a Finals appearance in 2007. He won back-to-back NBA MVPs in 2009 and 2010. He led the Cavaliers to their second NBA Finals appearance in 2015 and their 2016 NBA Finals win. In 9 seasons with Cleveland, James has averaged 27 points, 7 rebounds, and 7 assists per game.

In his first NBA game in 2003, James put up 25 points.

James set a new Cavaliers single-game-points record in 2005 when he scored 56 points.

fun facts

#1 In his 9th season with Cleveland, James made 4,842 total rebounds.

#2 He has won four NBA MVPs and three NBA Finals MVPs.

#3 James has been on 10 All-NBA First Teams.

#4 He is a 12-time NBA All-Star.

In 2010, LeBron James became the 10th NBA player to win back-to-back MVP awards.

The Moment

 LeBron James averaged 25.1 points per game in the Cavaliers' 2007 playoff run. His was the highest average for the team.

The greatest moment in Cavaliers history came during the 2007 Eastern Conference Finals. The team won 50 games in 2006–07 and went into the 2007 Playoffs as the number-two seed. After beating the Washington Wizards and the New Jersey Nets, Cleveland faced the Detroit Pistons for the right to go to the 2007 NBA Finals.

The two teams split the first four games of the series. Game 5 was in Detroit, and the winner would take control of the series. In game 5, LeBron James refused to let the Cavaliers lose. James scored 48 points in the Cavs' 109–107 double-overtime win. He scored Cleveland's last 25 points of the game, including all 18 of the team's overtime points.

The Cavs took the series back to Cleveland with a chance to finish in game 6. Cleveland dominated Detroit in game 6 and went to the 2007 NBA Finals, the franchise's first title-round appearance. Game 5 in Detroit would be remembered as one of the NBA's most memorable performances.

Sasha Pavlovic played 203 minutes during the 2007 Eastern Conference Finals. It was the second-longest playing time of the series.

After defeating the Detroit Pistons, Cavaliers owner Dan Gilbert hoisted the Eastern Conference trophy for the first time in franchise history.

All-Time Records

192 Most Three-Pointers Made in a Season
Cavaliers sharpshooter Wesley Person set the single-season record for **three-pointers** made, with 192 in 1997–98.

209 Most Steals in a Season
During the 1986–87 season, Cleveland guard Ron Harper set the single-season record for **steals**, with 209.

60%

882

Most Assists in a Season

Cavs point guard Andre Miller set the single-season record for assists, with 882 in 2001–02.

666

Most Defensive Rebounds in a Season

In 1982–83, Cleveland forward Cliff Robinson set the single-season record for most defensive rebounds, with 666.

Highest Field Goal Percentage in a Season

Cleveland forward Tyrone Hill set the single-season record for highest field goal percentage when he made 60 percent of his shots in 1996–97.

11

Highest Rebounds Per Game Average in a Season

In 2003–04, Cavs power forward Carlos Boozer grabbed 11 rebounds per game, setting the single-season record for rebounds per game.

![Cleveland Cavaliers logo] # Timeline

Throughout the team's history, the Cavaliers have had many memorable events that have become defining moments for the team and its fans.

1970

The Cleveland Cavaliers enter into the NBA as an expansion franchise. The team begins play in the Eastern Conference in 1970–71.

1975–1976

Led by coach Bill Fitch, center Jim Chones, and forward Campy Russell, the Cavaliers win 49 games during the regular season. The team makes it to the playoffs for the first time and reaches the conference finals.

1970   **1980**   **1990**

1987

The team finishes its most successful season to date, winning 55 games, and earning its first Central Division title.

1988–1993

Wilkens leads the Cavs to five playoff appearances in six seasons, including the Eastern Conference Finals in 1992.

2003

Cleveland selects high school graduate LeBron James with the number one pick in the 2003 NBA Draft. James becomes the face of not only the Cavs, but also the NBA.

2010

LeBron James leaves the Cleveland Cavaliers as a free agent, stunning the entire city of Cleveland. Afterward, the team would struggle for several seasons.

2006–2007

Led by coach Mike Brown, James, forward Larry Hughes, and guard Eric Snow, the Cavaliers win 50 games during the regular season. In 2007, the team makes it to the NBA Finals for the first time.

2014

Cleveland makes a trade with the Minnesota Timberwolves for power forward Kevin Love.

2000　　**2010**　　**2020**

2014–2015

The team wins 53 games and makes it to the 2015 NBA Finals. This is the franchise's second trip to the title round. The Cavs lose in six games to the Golden State Warriors.

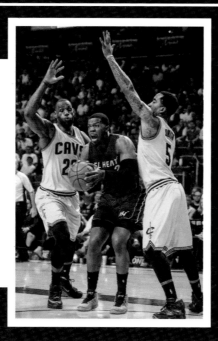

The Future

The Cavs are once again led by LeBron James. The team also has forward Kevin Love and guards Kyrie Irving and J.R. Smith as top scorers. Power forward Tristan Thompson gives the Cavaliers strong defense and rebounding. Cleveland aims to reach the NBA Finals once again.

Write a Biography

Life Story

A person's life story can be the subject of a book. This kind of book is called a biography. Biographies often describe the lives of people who have achieved great success. These people may be alive today, or they may have lived many years ago. Reading a biography can help you learn more about a great person.

Get the Facts

Use this book, and research in the library and on the internet, to find out more about your favorite star. Learn as much about this player as you can. What position does he play? What are his statistics in important categories? Has he set any records? Also, be sure to write down key events in the person's life. What was his childhood like? What has he accomplished off the court? Is there anything else that makes this person special or unusual?

Use the Concept Web

A concept web is a useful research tool. Read the questions in the concept web on the following page. Answer the questions in your notebook. Your answers will help you write a biography.

Concept Web

Your Opinion
- What did you learn from the books you read in your research?
- Would you suggest these books to others?
- Was anything missing from these books?

Adulthood
- Where does this individual currently reside?
- Does he or she have a family?

Childhood
- Where and when was this person born?
- Describe his or her parents, siblings, and friends.
- Did this person grow up in unusual circumstances?

Accomplishments off the Court
- What is this person's life's work?
- Has he or she received awards or recognition for accomplishments?
- How have this person's accomplishments served others?

Write a Biography

Help and Obstacles
- Did this individual have a positive attitude?
- Did he or she receive help from others?
- Did this person have a mentor?
- Did this person face any hardships?
- If so, how were the hardships overcome?

Accomplishments on the Court
- What records does this person hold?
- What key games and plays have defined his career?
- What are his stats in categories important to his position?

Work and Preparation
- What was this person's education?
- What was his or her work experience?
- How does this person work?
- What is the process he or she uses?

Trivia Time

Take this quiz to test your knowledge of the Cleveland Cavaliers.
The answers are printed upside down under each question.

1 Where do the Cavaliers currently play their home games?

A. Quicken Loans Arena

2 When did the team draft LeBron James?

A. 2003

3 How many times have the Cavaliers been to the NBA Finals?

A. Three

4 How many three-pointers did Wesley Person make in 1997–98?

A. 192

5 What position did Mark Price play?

A. Point Guard

6 When did the Cavaliers franchise make its first NBA Finals appearance?

A. 2007

7 Where did Brad Daugherty go to college?

A. The University of North Carolina at Chapel Hill

8 Who has the highest field goal percentage in a season?

A. Tyrone Hill

9 Where did Zydrunas Ilgauskas play before coming to the NBA?

A. Lithuania

10 How many assists did Andre Miller have in 2001–02?

A. 882

11 What is the name of the Cavaliers' mascot?

A. Moondog

12 When was the Cavs first NBA season?

A. 1970

Key Words

All-Star: a mid-season game made up of the best-ranked players in the NBA. A player can be named an All-Star and then be sent to play in this game.

assists: a statistic that is attributed to up to two players of the scoring team who shoot, pass, or deflect the ball toward the scoring teammate

blocks: when a defensive player taps an offensive player's shot out of the air and stops it from getting to the basket

conference: an association of sports teams that play each other

franchise: a team that is a member of a professional sports league

free agent: a player who is not under contract and free to sign with any team he or she wishes

playoffs: a series of games that occur after regular season play

rebounds: taking possession of the ball after missed shots

steals: taking possession of the ball from the other team

three-pointers: shots that count for three points, taken from behind the three-point line

Index

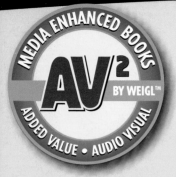

Log on to www.av2books.com

AV[2] by Weigl brings you media enhanced books that support active learning. Go to www.av2books.com, and enter the special code found on page 2 of this book. You will gain access to enriched and enhanced content that supplements and complements this book. Content includes video, audio, weblinks, quizzes, a slide show, and activities.

AV[2] Online Navigation

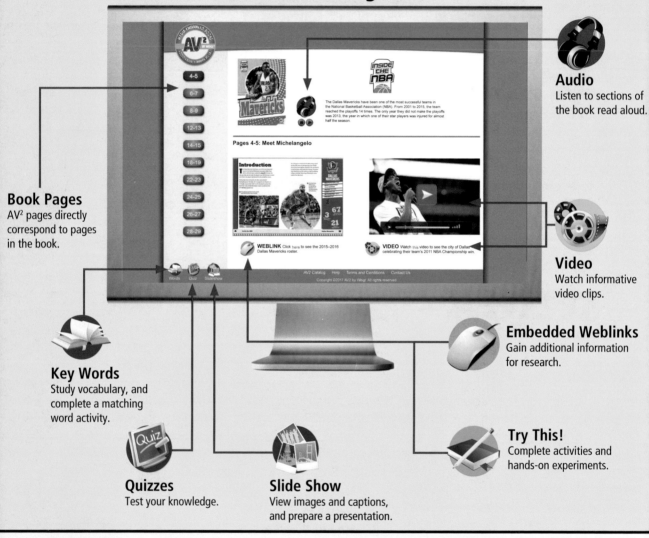

Audio
Listen to sections of the book read aloud.

Book Pages
AV[2] pages directly correspond to pages in the book.

Video
Watch informative video clips.

Key Words
Study vocabulary, and complete a matching word activity.

Embedded Weblinks
Gain additional information for research.

Try This!
Complete activities and hands-on experiments.

Quizzes
Test your knowledge.

Slide Show
View images and captions, and prepare a presentation.

AV[2] was built to bridge the gap between print and digital. We encourage you to tell us what you like and what you want to see in the future.

Sign up to be an AV[2] Ambassador at www.av2books.com/ambassador.